The
Little Book
of Abuse

The
Little Book
of Abuse

Jasmine Birtles

BⓍXTREE

First published 2000 by Boxtree
an imprint of Macmillan Publishers Ltd
25 Eccleston Place London SW1W 9NF
Basingstoke and Oxford

www.macmillan.com

Associated companies throughout the world

ISBN 0 7522 7236 5

Copyright © 2000 Jasmine Birtles

7 9 8 6

A CIP catalogue record for this book is available from
the British Library.

Designed by Nigel Davies
Printed by Omnia Books Ltd, Glasgow

Oi stupid! Read this book! If you don't you are a complete and utter snot-faced, pustulous invertebrate who doesn't deserve a life, let alone friends. A mollusc with learning difficulties could tell that this is the only book to buy if you have any sort of brain. It's packed with sharp, witty and downright offensive comebacks to jumped-up, smart-arse so-called friends and colleagues who try to get one over on you. Use any of these lines against them and you can tell them that it's not that you're being rude. They're just insignificant. Oh, and do write and tell me what you think of this book. If I've offended just one person with these lines I'll have done my job.

At the beautician, do you use the
emergency entrance?

She fell out of the ugly tree

and hit every branch

on the way down.

Look at him.

Living proof that Care in the

Community doesn't work.

You're a real action man: crew cut,
realistic scar, no genitals.

Uh oh. A couple of clowns short of
the full circus, aren't we?

Now do you see what happens when
cousins marry?

Your intellect is rivalled only by
gardening tools.

Not the brightest crayon
in the box, are we?

I can hardly contain my
indifference.

I'm not taking advice
from you.
You can't count to twenty-one
unless you're naked.

When they made you
they broke the mould . . .
but some of it grew back.

If I want to hear the
pitter-patter of tiny feet,
I'll put shoes on my cat.

As an outsider,

how do you view the human race?

You look familiar.

Didn't I dissect you in biology?

When I want your opinion,

I'll give it to you.

Have a drink with you?

I'd rather suture my own boils.

Make yourself at home!

Clean my kitchen.

Do I look like a people person?

You! Off my planet!!

I like children too.
Let's swap recipes.

Did the aliens

forget to remove

your anal probe?

Why don't you go home
and tell your mother
she wants you?

And your cry-baby,

snotty-nosed

opinion would be . . . ?

22

I'm not mad,
I've just been in a very bad mood
for thirty years.

Do they ever shut up
on your planet?

Whatever kind of look you were
going for, you missed.

Sarcasm is just

one more service we offer.

Are those your eyeballs?

I found them in my cleavage.

I'm not your type.

I'm not inflatable.

I'm trying to imagine you

with a personality.

Back off!

You're standing in my aura.

Don't worry.

I forgot your name, too!

How many times
do I have to flush
before you go away?

I just want revenge.

Is that so wrong?

You say I'm a bitch
like it's a bad thing.

I never forget a face and I can

remember both of yours.

Macho Law forbids me from

admitting I'm wrong.

Nice perfume.

Must you marinate in it?

Too many freaks,
not enough circuses.

Just smile and say:
'Yes, Mistress.'

Chaos, panic,

and disorder —

my work here is done.

Mummy, I want

to grow up to be a

neurotic bitch just like you.

Everyone thinks

I'm psychotic, except for my friends

deep inside the earth.

Did I mention

the kick in the groin you'll be

receiving if you touch me?

You look like shit.

Is that the style now?

Is it time for your medication

or mine?

And which dwarf

are you?

How do I set a laser pointer

to stun?

If I said anything to
offend it was
purely intentional.

Do you know, I went
through the bargain bin
and didn't see that one.

Have you got a minute?

Tell me everything you know.

Earth is full.

Go home.

Gene Police!
Get out of the pool!!

That's a fun outfit —
it's fancy dress, right?

Men have feelings too.

But hey,

who cares?

Nice dress.
Are you hoping
to slim into it?

Don't piss me off!

I'm running out of places

to hide the bodies.

What a pretty maternity dress . . .

you're not . . .

oh well.

Next mood swing:

six minutes.

I don't believe in miracles.

I rely on them.

48

He is so ugly they printed

his face on airline sick bags.

I'm busy. You're ugly.

Have a nice day.

Speak up! You're entitled

to your own stupid opinion.

I hate everybody,
and you're next.

And your completely

irrelevant point is . . . ?

I used to be schizophrenic,

but we're OK now.

Warning:

I have an attitude and

I know how to use it.

Of course I

don't look busy,

I did it right the first time.

Why do people
with closed minds always
open their mouths?

I'm multi-talented:
I can talk and piss you off
at the same time.

Do **not** start with me.

You will **not** win.

How can I miss you

if you won't go away?

All stressed out
and no one to choke.

You're one of those bad things
that happen to good people.

You have the right

to remain silent,

so please

SHUT UP.

If we are

what we eat,

you're fast,

cheap and easy.

You, David Mellor,
Michael Winner – in an ugly
competition who'd win?

I heard you
had a thought once
but it died of loneliness.

I'm so happy
I could kill.

Sorry if I looked interested.
I'm not.

Well, this day was a
total waste of make-up.

I'm not your type.
I have a pulse.

I don't know what
your problem is,
but I'll bet it's hard
to pronounce.

What would I do
without you —
apart from
be happy.

You've got all the personality
of a wet wick on bonfire night.

Please, keep talking.
I need the sleep.

Yes, it looks like a willy,

but smaller.

I'll try being nicer

if you'll try being smarter.

Go out with you?

How about never?

Is **never** good for you?

70

I see you've set aside
this special time to humiliate
yourself in public.

I'm really easy
to get along with once
you learn to worship me.

I'm out of my mind,

but feel free

to leave a message.

It sounds like English,
but I can't understand a word
you're saying.

I can see your point,
but I still think
you're full of shit.

I like you.

You remind me of when I was

young and stupid.

You are validating

my inherent mistrust

of strangers.

I have plenty of talent

and vision.

I just don't give a damn.

I'm already visualizing

the duct tape

over your mouth.

I will always cherish
the initial misconceptions
I had about you.

Thank you. We're all
refreshed and challenged
by your unique point of view.
NOW GET OUT!

The fact that no one
understands you doesn't mean
you're an artist.

Any connection between
your reality and mine is
purely coincidental.

What am I?
Flypaper for freaks?!

I'm not being rude.
You're just insignificant.

You sound reasonable . . .

time to increase the medication.

Does your train of thought

have a dining car?

Errors have been made.
Others will be blamed.

See, you should never
drink on an empty head.

He'd be out of his depth
in a car park puddle.

He's not so much of a has-been
as a definitely won't be.

You have delusions
of adequacy.

She has the wisdom of youth
and the energy of old age.

You're depriving a village
somewhere of an idiot.

There's nothing wrong with you that
reincarnation wouldn't cure.

Nice girl.

If she had two more legs

she could star in a Western.

I'd like to say something
nice about you but you
haven't paid me enough.

He's a man of few words —

but not few enough.

Can I buy you a drink,

or do you just want the money?

So I'm slow. You're ugly,
but do I ever mention it?

Are you usually this stupid or are
you just having a blond moment?

I may not be the best-looking
guy here, but I'm the
only one talking to you.

Just because you smell
like an ape it doesn't mean
you're Tarzan.

Nice girl —

has a face like a

cobbler's thumb.

Is that your face
or are you trying it out
for an ugly sister?

It must be a thrill for you
to know someone who
wears underwear.

Wow, you've been hit
really hard with
the ugly stick.

You're like a dot.com empire –
flash, empty and
a disappointment to millions.

Is that a goatee

or has a bird just crapped

on your chin?

Nice hair.

Was it that shape

when you bought it?

I just don't
hate myself enough
to go out with you.

Please don't try
and kiss me –
I'll only laugh.

You're so dull
you couldn't entertain
a doubt.

You've got the personality
of a dial tone.

You're not paranoid.
Everyone **does** hate you.

She has the face of a saint —

a St Bernard.

His nose is so big

he can smell the future.

Is that your nose

or are you growing

a third arm?

I like you –
but then I've never
had any taste.

She's got a face like a
smacked arse.

He doesn't act stupid,
it's the real thing.

One more facelift and
you'll have a beard.

Go on, I know you like me —
I can see your tail wagging.

I'm fond of him,
but not as much as he is.

The less I see you
the more I like you.

Use your brain.

It's the little things that count.

If ignorance is bliss,

why aren't you happy?

He won't bore you
with a long speech —
he can do it with a short one.

I've never seen anything
as ugly as you without
paying admission.

You'll never be
as old
as you look.

Taste?
I've seen crab
dressed better.

He's not
himself today,
thankfully.

Oh, please save your breath

to blow up your

girlfriend tonight.

You'll never make
Who's Who but you might
get into **What's That**.

Her face bears

the imprint of the last man

who sat on it.

Would you mind standing
downwind?

Be reasonable.

Do it my way.

123

Since I gave up hope
I feel much better.

I've had a lot to drink,
and you're beginning to look
human.

If you don't go away
and leave me alone I'll find
someone who will.

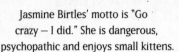

Jasmine Birtles' motto is "Go crazy — I did." She is dangerous, psychopathic and enjoys small kittens. She was once arrested at the Moulin Rouge nightclub over an incident involving three ping pong balls and a length of rubber tubing. She was charged under Act Three, paragraph four of *The Mousetrap* and was sentenced to 400 hours community service as a cellist in the BBC Symphony Orchestra. She has an irrational fear of radishes and if placed in a nursery garden will attack at random. She was once found in a country lane staring wildly and brandishing a shot gun and hand-written sign which read "Pick your own — go on, try! Just try!" She is wanted in 17 countries for prune-trafficking and obtaining cheese with menaces.

I never forget a face but in your
case I'm willing to make an
exception.